Foreword

No, I don't presume you are an idiot. But if you are, this book should still be able to help you attain a well-rounded understanding of effective crime prevention for the home. Though introducing newer concepts like Crime Prevention Through Environmental Design, it also covers all of the more familiar basics of home security. It's a "how-to" book that will reduce your fear of crime while making your home more safe and secure.

What you don't know can hurt you. Knowledge of Crime Prevention is a prime example. That very important body of information is unknown to most as it is kept a virtual secret. Crime Prevention is not taught to children, students, worshippers, soldiers, or even cops. This results in many unnecessary victims of property crimes and violent assaults.

Another big unknown to the general public is the large number of evil predators among us. Most people don't want to think about that or their own personal vulnerability. Only a small percentage of us perceive this reality and know the level of ever-present danger. It's cops, paramedics, firefighters, and emergency room personnel who see the mayhem and victims of crime on a regular basis. The rest of the population lives in blissful ignorance and complacency until such time as they may become victims themselves.

Police can't be everywhere at all times. In many parts of the USA, they are encouraged to be nowhere at all. Police defunding has had predictable results with crime in many areas is quickly rising. No one is immune to the threat of criminal victimization. Personal diligence is required to maximize your safety and you must protect yourself. But how? Fortunately, there have been a lot of advancements in strategy, tactics, and technology, focused on effectively preventing crime. CPTED being chief among them. Crime Prevention Through Environmental Design. It's a big-picture synergetic solution. The pages ahead will offer you a comprehensive body of information and actions that you can take, including traditional solutions, to protect your family and your property.

You will likely come to view the environment around you differently as the pages ahead will expand the horizon of your situational awareness. You'll attain a confident understanding of how to achieve much greater safety and security. The process and

tactics are simple and easy to comprehend. Come on in and let's get

started!

Chapter One

CPTED PRINCIPLES

Crime Prevention Through Environmental Design (CPTED) is a multi-disciplinary approach for reducing crime and fear of crime. CPTED strategies aim to reduce victimization, deter offender decisions that precede criminal acts, and build a sense of community among inhabitants so they can gain territorial control of areas to reduce crime opportunities.

It can be combined with traditional crime prevention approaches including locks, gates, alarms, cameras and lighting. Effective and visually pleasing security solutions are achieved. CPTED can be applied without interfering with the normal use of your home. It is easy to apply and often economical to implement.

THE FOUR PRINCIPLES OF CPTED ARE:

Natural Surveillance

Natural Access Control

Territorial Reinforcement

Maintenance and Management

There are strong overlaps and synergies among the four CPTED principles. These have been identified separately for convenience and clarity of understanding. In practice, it may be useful to see all four principles as different facets of a single technique for dealing with the security of the physical environment. Good CPTED creates a perception among offenders that there is an enhanced risk in selecting your home as a target.

Natural surveillance

The fundamental premise is that criminals do not wish to be observed. Surveillance by legitimate observers increases the perceived risk to offenders. This may also increase the actual risk to offenders if those observing are willing to act when potentially threatening situations develop.

So, the primary aim of surveillance is not to keep intruders out (although it may have that result) but rather, to keep intruders under observation. Natural surveillance can be achieved by a number of techniques. Windows, lighting and the removal of obstructions can improve sight lines and increase surveillance.

The ability to see and be seen is a key element to your safety at home. You want to be able to spot a potential threat before it's in your face.

1. There should be a clear line of sight between the street and your front door.

2. Windows should not be covered by blinds or curtains.

3. Fences should not block your view, so avoid privacy fencing.

4. No bushes should be taller than 2 feet and tree canopy should descend no lower than six feet. This offers a 4-foot swath of clear and unobstructed views.

In addition to threats to you or your property, you can also help to keep an eye on activities on the street and your neighbor's property if your line of sight is unobstructed.

OK. You understand why you want to see what's around you but why do you need to be seen by others? The reason is that most people are honest and law abiding. Your neighbors and other people passing by your home have eyes that you can utilize to enhance your security. Imagine that a burglar is in your back yard and trying to kick in your back door. If your fencing is chain link or wrought iron, your neighbors may spot them and call the police. That ability for others to see unwanted activity in your back yard may discourage a criminal from targeting your home. Conversely, intruders are emboldened if they find themselves within a privacy fenced in area as they can't be seen or identified.

Police patrols and others passing by your home can offer you added protection by confirming that everything is normal within your residence, if sightlines are open. If they glance at your living room window and see you being duck taped up by armed intruders, they may take action to get you the help you need. If all they can see is curtains or closed blinds, then you are failing to take advantage of the all-important attributes of natural surveillance.

Positive activity generators are another way to let potential bad actors know that you have eyes on their presence, anything that involves you or family members in safe activity outside your home enhances your observations of the nearby neighborhood. Rocking chairs on the porch, mowing the lawn, walking the dog, tending the garden, etc..

In an emergency when seconds count, little things can mean a lot. One of the biggest impediments to a quick emergency response is the inability to locate the address where the first responders are needed. Large reflective house numbers that are easily seen from the street are a very helpful addition that will enhance your overall security.

Will I be seen? That is a question asked by all burglars. The better your natural surveillance and the more human activity which criminals see, will be factors that discourage them from burglarizing your residence.

Natural Access Control

Natural access control relies on doors, fences, shrubs, and other physical elements to keep unauthorized persons out of a particular place if they do not have a legitimate reason for being there.

In its most elementary form, access control can be achieved at your home by the use of adequate locks, doors and window barriers. If a target is seen as difficult, it may also be unattractive to potential criminals.

Because any strategy that fosters access control is also likely to impede movement, careful consideration should be given to access control strategies.

Territorial Reinforcement

People naturally protect a territory that they feel is their own and have a certain respect for the territory of others. Clear boundaries between public and private areas achieved by using physical elements such as fences, good maintenance and landscaping are ways to express ownership.

Identifying intruders is much easier in such well-defined spaces. Territorial reinforcement can be seen to work when a space, by its clear legibility, transparency, and directness, discourages potential offenders because of neighbors familiarity with each other and the surroundings.

Maintenance and Management

This is related to the home indicating 'pride of place' and territorial reinforcement. The less well-maintained residence is more likely to attract criminal activities. The maintenance and the 'image' of your home can have a major impact on whether it will become

targeted. Good maintenance is known to reduce all types of crimes.

- Mow your lawn.

- Trim the bushes.

- Trim the trees.

- Thin out any wooded areas.

- Repair lighting fixtures.

- Repair any broken fencing.

- Pick up trash on a regular basis.

- Store tools. If in a shed - keep it locked.

- Remove fallen trees and limbs.

- Paint the home or repair any damaged vinyl siding.

- Replace or repair the roof if needed.

Chapter Two

WINDOWS

Always **keep your windows locked** at all times. Never open them more than 5" and only then if they are pinned or otherwise locked to restrict further opening. 24/7.

Most burglars enter through doors. About 65% break in through the front door, back door or garage. Windows, especially those on the ground floor are a burglar's second choice for illegal entry. Protecting your windows is essential to your home security.

Some Types of Windows and How to Make Them Secure

Double Hung windows, often found on older homes, tend to be the most vulnerable to break-ins. They have two glass panes, one above the other and are often secured with a crescent latch.

The latch will usually not be designed for good security. It just keeps the window closed. A crescent latch can be easily defeated by inserting a knife or other flat tool. Also, the latches are subject to failure, as the windows may not close properly when they swell over time due to hot weather. In older homes it's common to see latches painted over so many times that they can no longer secure the window.

The solution is pin locks. They are large pins that fit in a window frame to keep it closed. They work with double hung, single hung and slider type windows.

All you need to install a pin lock is a drill and some screws. Install the chain on the window frame and then drill a hole for the pin.

Casement Windows

Two types of casement windows:

TYPE A: Hinged on the side and cranks or swings outward.

TYPE B: Hinged at the top and swings outward.

A burglar can break out the window in the area of the crank then reach in and crank open the window. If the window is partially open, the screen may be cut or removed, again giving the burglar access to the crank to open the window far enough to make illegal entry.

You'll want to inspect your window hardware. If your push bar or operator is worn out, it should be replaced. Make sure it's sturdy enough that if your window is cranked open a few inches, a burglar won't be able to force the window open to gain entry - at least not without breaking the window or window frame.

Few burglars force open casement windows if it means breaking the glass. Burglars hate making loud noises. Breaking windows alerts the whole neighborhood to their presence. Also broken glass may result in them getting cut and bleeding which leaves DNA evidence.

Securing casement windows is difficult, especially thin gauge aluminum casement windows commonly found on cheaply constructed homes. To secure these windows you may have to replace them.

Jalousie (Louvered) Windows

This type of window is often found in bathrooms and kitchens in older homes. The individual panes can be easily broken in or in some cases simply removed by sliding them out of the frame.

The panels can be forced open easily.

To prevent someone from removing the panes of glass

you can glue them in. However, that's not going to stop someone

from breaking them. If ventilation is not critical you may want to

replace it with a storm window, or a double hung window.

Like to open your windows to ventilate your home?

Don't open them more than 5' or unwanted visitors may climb

through the opening. To keep burglars from raising an open window further you can utilize a track lock (see below) on sliding windows

or a pin lock on double hung or single hung windows.

Window film, laminated glass and bullet resistant glass

are options to consider. Whatever your window type be sure to keep

it locked at all times. If opened, remember to secure it so that it can't

be opened more than 5 inches. Be sure to use them for their

surveillance value. Leave them unblocked by curtains and blinds

whenever possible.

Chapter Three

DOORS AND LOCKS

First and foremost, I can't stress enough how important it is to keep your doors **locked and deadbolted** at all times. They should only be unlocked during times that authorized people are passing through. 24/7. Locks do no good if they are not used and many times burglars simply enter through unlocked doors.

Generally speaking, deadbolts are sturdy locks that can withstand a kick in and other forced entry attempts. However, a door with a deadbolt can still be kicked down if the door itself is not solid. So, to protect your door against kick in, you want to make sure that both the lock and door are of high-quality grade.

Because steel is so strong, a steel door is the most secure option. Your second most secure selection is a solid wood door. Anything less than steel or solid wood will not afford the best security. Windows in entry doors are problematic because they can be broken which can enable a burglar to easily enter. A peephole with a wide viewing aspect is a very good as you want to be able to identify visitors without unlocking the door. Video doorbells will be discussed in the CAMERAS chapter.

Reinforce your door's weak spot, the jamb, with a heavy-duty strike plate cover. Use extra-long screws in all the door lock hardware. Look at your existing screws in the door lock. They are likely less than 1" long. Replace them with 3" screws which will make your doors much more kick in resistant. It's a cheap adjustment that can make all the difference in a burglary attempt.

Sliding Glass doors present their own challenges. The bar alone, placed in the track, will not afford adequate protection.

That's because sliding glass doors are particularly vulnerable to break ins. In most cases all an intruder has to do is lift the door off the tracks. This will usually allow them to gain entrance, even if the door was locked, since the standard lock on the doors is usually nothing more than a latch.

An easy fix is to place several screws vertically in the top track that protrude into the space between the top of the door and the top track. Properly installed, they will still allow the door to slide but will prevent it from being lifted from the track by a burglar.

You may also wish to add shatterproof film to the glass. Finally, glass break detection is an option on most alarm systems.

Garage doors. Should always be locked. (Note that the connecting door from the garage to the home is an exterior door that should be at least solid wood and have a deadbolt installed.)

If you have a garage door opener it presents another easy way for a burglar to gain entry. In less than six seconds with nothing more than a wire hanger inserted at the top-middle of the garage door they can catch the cord and trigger the emergency release latch.

Cut the handle off just above the emergency release cord.

You will still be able to pull the cord, but a hanger inserted by a

burglar seeking the handle with the bent end of the hanger, to unlock

the garage, will fail.

Another effective burglary technique with the hanger inserted above the door is to hook the lever directly which will unlock the door. Insert a small zip tie (one that can still be broken with the pull cord in an emergency) between the hole with the cord and a hole in the moving part of the track directly above it. A hanger will slip off the lever rather than catching and unlocking the door. Google search "breaking into a garage door in six seconds" if you want to watch a video showing the vulnerability.

Remotes and built-in car remotes are easy ways for a burglar to enter your garage door. Never leave your garage door remote in your car. Also, we are not in favor of the built-in garage door opener buttons in some new cars. You may not wish to activate that feature. Remember to keep your car locked at all times, even if it is in the garage. Never leave valuables visible in the vehicle. Never leave a gun in a car.

Finally, no doggie doors please. But if you must have one make sure it's too small for a child to enter. Burglars will send children in to open the door for their adult partners in crime.

Chapter Four

CAMERAS

Cameras for home security have achieved a lot of advancements that have all benefitted the homeowner. They are more affordable and offer many features not available previously. More is better with cameras as they allow you to have more coverage of your property.

There are many do it yourself options and more traditional security company installed systems. Do your research and you'll likely be pleased with the results. Some systems combine cameras with more comprehensive burglar alarm notification. This chapter focuses on cameras.

Features that you will want to consider are:

- Fast motion activation You want a camera that works fast and doesn't hesitate.

- Intuitive smartphone app.

- High-Definition video.

- Night Vision.

- Cameras combined with lights.

- Cloud Video Storage.

- Good field of view.

You may not want to purchase all of the cameras at one time. It may be more affordable to build out your system over time. If do it yourself is your choice, then pick a company that will allow you to add to the system with compatible components that ultimately achieve all of your proposed requirements. Some systems require a subscription to unlock advanced features.

Start with a video doorbell. If you have only one camera, it is your best choice. They allow you to see people in your front yard and get alerts on your phone when people are there or if they ring the doorbell. Better yet, you can talk to them without having to go to the door. Even if you are halfway around the world you can interact with persons at your door, and they will think you are home. That adds extra protection as burglars almost never want to break into a home that they believe is occupied. They can operate by doorbell power or be battery operated. Look for a field of view of at least 120 degrees. In my opinion, video doorbells are the single biggest advancement in home security in recent times.

Next you may want to add a dedicated camera for your driveway. Especially if that is where your cars are parked. Car burglary is a very common offense and a camera there with a spotlight that is activated by motion can go a long way to keep burglars out of your vehicles.

Third, you may want a back door camera. It should give you some back yard coverage as well. It's also a good location for a motion activated spotlight. Keep in mind that you can also set up audio alerts for each camera. I use unique sounds for each camera in my system so that I'm instantly aware which camera has been activated.

Chapter Five

ALARMS

The best alarm system will fit your budget and have the devices and features you need and want to protect your home. There are both do it yourself and professional vendor options. Here is what you should look for when buying a home security system.

- **Price:** You can expect to pay for equipment and professional monitoring. Additional fees for installation and professional monitoring may apply.

- **Contracts:** The average contract length is 3 years but there are many home security providers that have no contract options.

- **Monitoring Options:** Choose between professional and self-monitoring for your system.

- **Equipment: Basics:** A control panel or hub, or smart phone control.

- **Detection Devices:** Window contacts, door contacts, motion detectors, glass break sensors, cameras, video doorbells, etc.

- **Smart Home Integrations:** Products like smart lights, locks, climate control, fire/smoke/carbon monoxide detectors, etc.

- **Mobile App Access:** Make sure you have remote access and control by mobile app, allowing you to arm, disarm and manage smart devices.

Be sure to include signs that show you are protected by an alarm system. Even if you don't have an alarm, it's good to display a sign indicating that you are protected by one. Remember that you can always start simple and add on as you can afford to expand.

Chapter Six

LIGHTING

Indoor lighting can deter burglars from breaking in, but they often break in anyway after knocking on the door to see if anyone answers. Outdoor security lighting is effective if there are people - neighbors, pedestrians or police to actually see suspicious activity.

That said, outdoor lighting has several benefits. It helps keep you safe when you are leaving or arriving at your home at night. You can more easily see your path of travel and it illuminates any unwanted visitors that may be otherwise lurking undetected in the darkness.

It works nicely with your cameras in that LED outdoor lights throw a clear white light that offers accurate color rendition.

Video recorded is more likely to be clear and it will be easier to describe the true colors of clothing. Lighting should illuminate pathways, your front porch, driveway and yard. Continuous lighting with overlapping cones of light during hours of darkness is preferable. You may wish to include motion activated lights or spotlight cams integrated with your alarm system on the corners of your house.

Different applications of light call for different levels of brightness. The era of incandescent bulbs is gone and the lighting technology that has surpassed it is the LED bulb. LED is superior because of its long life and extremely low power consumption. Lumens have substituted for watts to become the new light measurement because a bulb with higher wattage doesn't mean it will produce a brighter light. To tailor the performance of a light to the purpose for which it is intended you can refer to the values in the following guide.

1. Path Lighting   100 - 200 lumens

2. Step Lights   12 - 100 lumens

3. Flood Lights   700 - 1300 lumens

4. Motion Sensor Lights   300 - 700 lumens

5. Pond/Pool Lights   200 - 400 lumens

6. Lights on Walls   50 - 185 lumens

7. Landscape   50 - 300 lumens

Burglars don't want to be seen. Lighting dovetails nicely with natural surveillance while enhancing pedestrian safety and can be an attractive addition to your home as well. Since all good security strategies are layered, you should also consider placing some of the interior lights on timers. They help to give the home an "occupied" look while you are away on vacation. Many smart apps will allow you to manually trigger lights on or off as well.

Chapter Seven

LANDSCAPING

Whether you realize it or not, your yard is an advertisement. It gives passers-by an indication of your home's value. It also signals the potential ease or difficulty for entry to a burglar. Landscape is a key factor when criminals case your house. It helps let them know how hard it would be to break in, how long it would take and even where they should start. Ultimately, effective prevention boils down to one thing - visibility. Landscape design, like lighting, is a great way to maximize an intruder's chance of being seen which all burglars know can lead to capture and imprisonment. Bad for business for those whose profession is home burglary.

Support natural surveillance by observing the 2' 6' rule. No bushes higher than 2' and no descending tree canopy lower than 6'. This creates a 4-foot swath of clear and unobstructed view. It allows you to see threats at a distance and eliminates ambush points.

Trimming shrubbery isn't fun. Need an incentive? The more dense and unruly your bushes, the easier it is for thieves to find a hiding spot. Windows and doors obscured by shrubs are particularly vulnerable points of illegal entry. By keeping your bushes neat, tidy and short, your windows and doors are no longer appealing targets. If a criminal attempts a break in, there's a good chance they will be seen by you, someone nearby and possibly your security cameras.

Make use of thorns or "hostile vegetation." Popular choices like rose bushes and holly provide both protection and beauty. They add a nice pop of color and will prick and puncture anyone who comes too close. They are good selections for plants nearby windows for example. If potential intruders notice these painful plants, they are less likely to attempt an entryway.

Amplify sound with gravel. Silence is the friend of a burglar. Dense grass and paved walkways dramatically reduce the sound of incoming footsteps. Loose rocks and gravel, however, will only make their movements more noticeable. Every step has the potential to blow their cover and that can be enough for thieves to look elsewhere.

You may wish to use plants or low bushes to direct visitors along a pathway to your front door. Good landscaping helps to show people where they are supposed to go. It also enhances territoriality which shows not only ownership but that you take pride in your property. When implemented with other security measures, strategic landscaping is a painless way to enhance your overall protection.

Chapter Eight

FENCES

Fences land in the "Territoriality" and "Natural Access Control" areas of CPTED principles. They show your property boundaries and are a clear border between public and semi-private spaces. Fencing your entire yard and with gates leading to the back, through the side yards, is a good security measure. Fence height is not as important a factor as the type of fence selected. Chain link or wrought iron are two good choices. CPTED fencing is any fencing that you can clearly see through.

Avoid privacy fencing. Why? Remember Natural Surveillance? The ability to see and be seen. That is ever so important to good security. Privacy fencing creates an island of safety and security for a burglar who, for example, climbs a privacy fence (or walks through an unlocked gate) into your back yard. They are afforded their most wished for environment. One in which they will not be seen. Sure, you may have cameras back there but why tempt a burglar by utilizing a fence that will invite them to enter and explore ways to break into your house.

Worse yet, a privacy fence allows a criminal to perform a physical attack without being seen. You want to utilize the eyes of your law-abiding neighbors to help enhance both your personal security and the protection of your property. In addition, you are unable to have eyes on the neighbor's houses around you when you are sealed up behind a wooden wall. Don't surrender Natural Surveillance to a false sense of safety behind a privacy fence.

You might ask what a four-foot chain link or wrought iron fence is going to do to keep people out of my front yard? The answer is it will do a lot. Part of the thought process of the burglar is what they perceive as the risks involved to include how hard it will be to commit the crime unseen. Fences help deter thieves in several ways.

1. Fences mark property lines and show people that they belong outside the barrier.

2. A gate to the marked path leading to the doorway keeps visitors on an approved route and makes any wanderings to other areas of the yard noticeable as unusual and suspicious.

3. If someone climbs over a fence, they are obviously an unauthorized intruder and witnesses may call the police.

4. Fences show that you care about what happens on your property

and that you are likely paying attention to arrivals.

5. The side gates leading to the back yard should both be locked.

That forces an unauthorized intruder to climb over the fence,

thereby increasing their chance of being observed for their

suspicious activity.

6. Once in the back yard they can still be seen by neighbors

surrounding your property. Their ability to break into your

home unseen is also greatly diminished by the see-through

CPTED fencing.

Epilogue

What are your takeaways from this home safety publication? I trust you now see that there are many factors that influence the making of a safer home. Crime Prevention Through Environmental Design, when incorporated in your planning, will go a long way toward effectively securing your property. Criminals will seek to take advantage of weaknesses in your home's defenses. So, the best idea is to have no weaknesses. If your home presents a hard target, it is likely to deter a burglar. Crime prevention techniques are focused on eliminating or minimizing the opportunity for a crime to occur.

Perhaps you are already well along the way to implementing good practices as described in this manual. But some of the best practices described may be cost prohibitive or maybe you have a lot to do to improve your security. It all might seem like too much to accomplish. Just do it a little bit at a time. Things like longer screws in door hardware are surely an affordable adjustment. So are placing protruding screws in the upper track of a sliding glass door to keep the doors from being lifted out of the tracks. Trimming hedges and low hanging tree canopy are also goals that can be achieved with just a little investment of time. Do the more costly items in order of importance or affordability as you are able.

This booklet was designed as a short read, covering a lot of conceptual territory, while offering practical advice on making your home a safer place. There are no guarantees of safety in life. Fortunately, you have complete control over the protection plans that you employ to deter an offender from attempting to target your home. If you adhere to the best practices for home safety, you will greatly improve your overall security while lessening the fear of crime.

About the Author

David is a crime prevention specialist with thousands of formal training hours. He is certified by the Florida Attorney General as a Crime Prevention Practitioner and Crime Prevention Through Environmental Design Practitioner. He regularly performs security surveys at homes, houses of worship, businesses, government agencies, industrial locations and military bases. He also instructs classes on situational awareness and a survival mindset.

Thousands have attended his seminars. David lives with his wife

Kathy in Pensacola, Florida where thousands live the way that

millions wish they could.

David Craig, FCPP, FCP

Please contact me with your comments or questions at

David@realityadvanced.com.